Contents

What is a habitat? 4

Rats all around 8

Cockroach restaurants 12

Sewer surprises 18

Big brown bats 20

Slimy snails and slugs 22

Follow a slug 28

Glossary 30

Find out more 31

Index 32

What is a habitat?

A **habitat** is a place where plants and animals can find what they need to live. What are those needs? Plants and animals need food, water, and shelter.

rat

5

Almost any place can be a **habitat**. You can find **sewers** under the streets. Sewers are filled with the dirty water from streets, houses, and toilets.

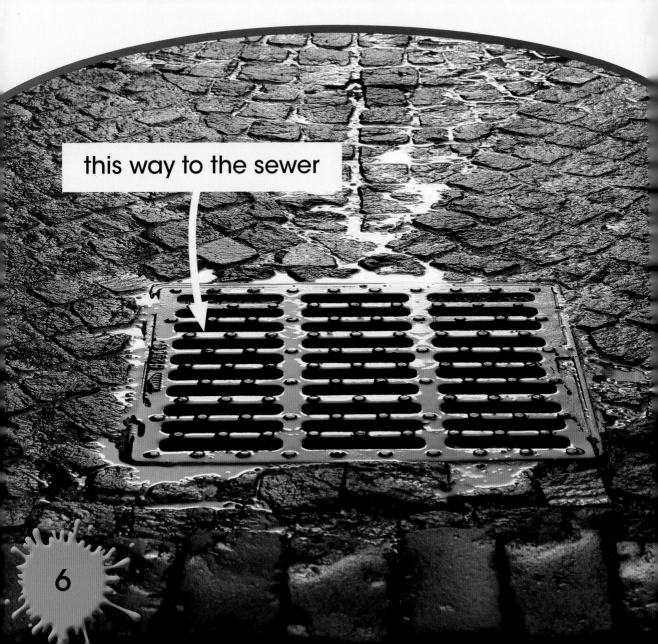

this way to the sewer

What could you find living in the dirty water and rotting leaves in this gutter?

A **gutter** is the tube that catches leaves and water from the roofs of houses. Even sewers and gutters are habitats!

7

Rats all around

Rats live everywhere people do. There are thousands and even millions of them in city **sewers**. Why? They can find lots of water and food down there.

Norway rat

These hungry rats are
searching for food.

nest

Rats often build their nests in places connected to **sewers**. They go into the sewer to find food.

10

FUN FACT

Some of a rat's favourite foods are human poo and ground-up food from kitchen sinks. They also like to eat dead rats and cockroaches.

Cockroaches are easy to find in **sewers**. They feed on dead and rotting plants and animals. That is exactly what they find down there. They also like to be in the dark, and it is always dark in the sewers!

These cockroaches are enjoying rotting kiwi fruit.

13

Cockroaches need to drink. They sometimes get water from toilets and dirty puddles. This is one reason they spread dirt and carry **diseases**.

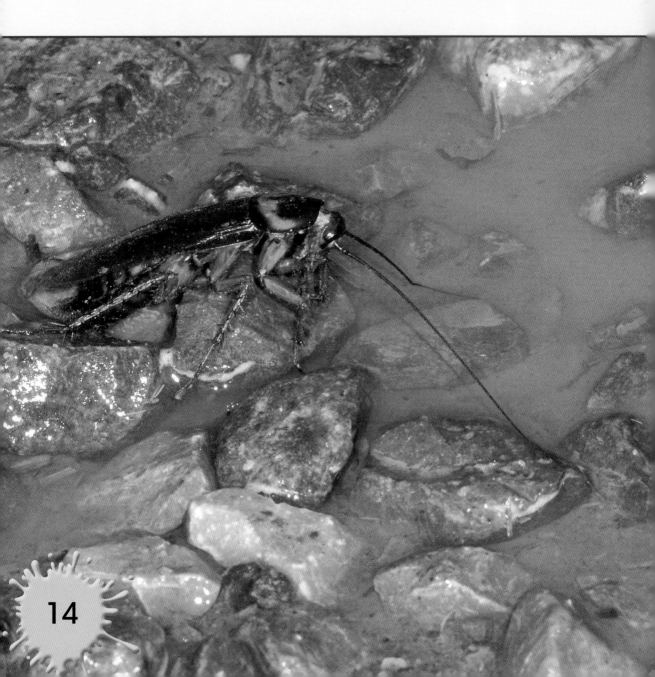

Lots of poo can be found in sewers. This cockroach is eating some!

poo

Cockroaches are insects. They have six legs and run very fast. They leave behind a trail of smelly, oily liquid. Other cockroaches like the smell and come running.

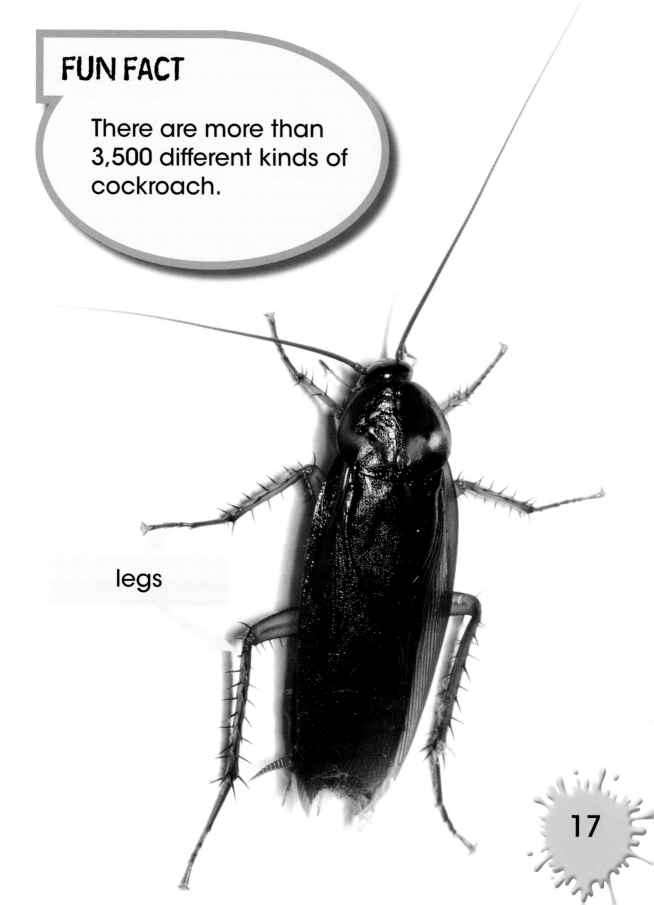

legs

Sewer surprises

Some people have unkindly flushed baby alligators down the toilet in the past. Anything that is flushed down a toilet travels to the **sewers**.

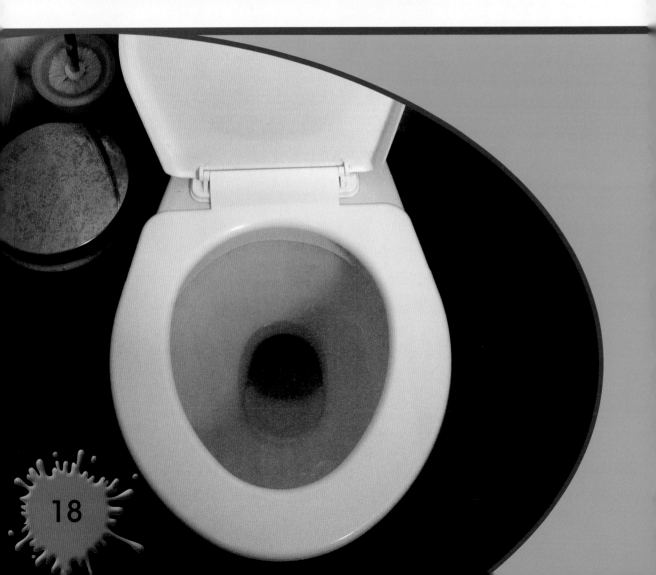

baby alligator

FUN FACT

Alligators have been found in sewers. Young alligators might be able to live in a sewer for a while by eating rats. It is unlikely that any fully grown alligators could be found in sewers today, though.

19

Big brown bats

Brown bats sometimes sleep for the winter in **sewers** and other dark underground places. This is called **hibernation**. They even sleep in graveyards.

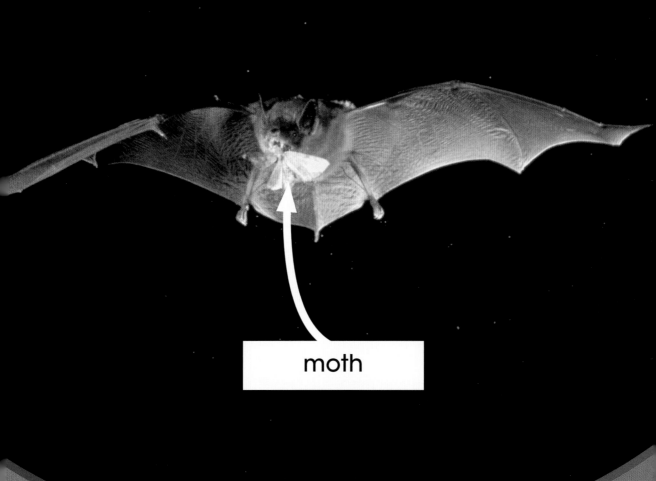

moth

FUN FACT

Brown bats fly out at night to look for insects to eat. They eat mosquitoes, beetles, and moths.

Slimy snails and slugs

You may find snails moving slowly around **gutters**. Snails' bodies make a lot of slime. This slime is so thick that it acts like a suction cup. The suction helps snails travel upside down!

FUN FACT

Snails move by creeping along on a flat foot underneath their bodies. Unlike us, snails only have one foot!

FUN FACT

Snails can't hear but they can feel vibrations.

Gutters also attract slugs. This is because slugs like to eat rotting plants and leaves. Just like snails, slugs are covered with a slime called **mucus**. Mucus keeps their skins **moist**, or slightly wet.

25

Slugs trail slime from their undersides.
This slime helps them slide along the
ground. They leave a trail of slime
behind them.

slug trail

FUN FACT

Slugs have holes in the sides of their bodies! A slug takes air into its body through this hole and the hole can open or close.

27

Follow a slug

What you need:
- your eyes
- an area where you can find slugs

What to do:

1. Go outside after it has rained and look around.

2. Find a slug and look for its slime trail.

3. How far back can you trace it? Can you see where it has been? Where do you think it might be going? Can you see the hole in its side?

29

Glossary

disease illness

gutter tube that catches water from the roofs of houses. Many rotting leaves get stuck in gutters, too.

habitat place where animals or plants live and grow

hibernation sleeping for a long time in winter, saving energy

moist slightly wet or damp

mucus slippery stuff that animals produce from their bodies

sewer place under the street where the dirty water from streets and houses goes

Find out more

Find out

Which snails are the fastest?

Books to read

Animal Neighbours: Rat, Stephen Savage (Wayland, 2007)

Bug Books: Cockroach, Karen Hartley, Chris Macro, and Philip Taylor (Heinemann Library, 2008)

Bug Books: Snail, Karen Hartley and Chris Macro (Heinemann Library, 2008)

Websites

http://www.bats.org.uk/pages/ batsforkids.html
This website has lots of information about how you can help save bat habitats.

http://www.geocities.com/sseagraves/ allaboutsnails.htm
This website is packed with snail facts and activities.

http://www.nhm.ac.uk/kids-only/life/life- small/cockroaches/
Find out some fascinating facts about cockroaches on this website.

31

Index

alligators 18–19

bats 20–21
blood-suckers 25

cockroaches 11, 12–17

dead animals 11, 12
dirty water 6, 7, 14
diseases 14

gutters 7, 22, 24

habitats 4, 6, 7
hibernation 20

mites 25
moths 21
mucus 24

nests 10

poo 11, 15

rats 8–11, 19
rotting food and plants 12, 24

sewers 6, 8, 10, 12, 18, 20
slime 22, 24, 26, 28
slugs 24–27
slugs, following 28–29
snails 22–23

toilets 6, 14, 18